GOVERNMENT
OF CANADA

FEDERAL GOVERNMENT

Edited by
Heather C. Hudak

Weigl

Published by Weigl Educational Publishers Limited
6325 10th Street S.E.
Calgary, AB T2H 2Z9
Website: www.weigl.com

Library and Archives Canada Cataloguing-in-Publication Data available upon request.
Fax (403) 233-7769 WEIGL for the attention of the Publishing Records department.

ISBN 978-1-55388-677-8 (hard cover)
ISBN 978-1-55388-681-5 (soft cover)

Printed in the United States of America in North Mankato, Minnesota
1 2 3 4 5 6 7 8 9 0 14 13 12 11 10

082010
WEP230610

Project Coordinator: Heather C. Hudak

Produced for Weigl Educational Publishers Inc. by RJF Publishing LLC
(www.RJFpublishing.com)
Project Editor: Emily Dolbear
Photo Research: Edward A. Thomas
Design: Tammy West/Westgraphix LLC

Weigl acknowledges Getty Images as its primary image supplier for this title.

Photo of David Johnston on page 17 is by Michael L. Davenport.

We gratefully acknowledge the financial support of the Government of Canada
through the Canada Book Fund for our publishing activities.

CONTENTS

Introduction to Canada's Government

Large groups of people need rules for each member to follow. Most countries, cities, and towns have a government for this purpose. Government also organizes large groups of people to accomplish things an individual could not do alone. Most governments, for example, make and enforce laws, collect taxes, construct roads and bridges, educate children, and provide for defence.

Many countries, such as Canada, have a democratic form of government. The words *democratic* and *democracy* come from the Greek words *demos*, or "people," and *kratos*, or "power." In other words, the people have power.

There are two forms of democracy: **direct democracy** and **representative democracy**. Direct democracy gives every citizen the right to vote on every issue. Athens and many other city-states in ancient Greece governed themselves in this way. Requiring citizens across a large country to gather, debate ideas, and vote on every issue is not practical, however.

Most democratic countries, including Canada, are representative democracies. Citizens elect representatives to attend meetings, vote on issues, and make laws for them. Each person has a voice in government by voting in elections. However, only a small group of representatives has the power to make decisions.

Canada has three levels of government. Each level of government has its own powers and responsibilities. The federal government controls matters common to all provinces and territories. Provincial and territorial governments handle matters that are unique to each province and territory. Municipal governments manage matters that affect individual cities, towns, villages, and other municipalities.

Athens, Greece, is generally considered the birthplace of democracy. In ancient times, slaves, women, and immigrants were not permitted to vote, however.

Think about it!

1. List three things your government does that you could not do alone.

2. Why do you think Canada is a representative rather than direct democracy?

3. Can you think of some advantages and disadvantages of having a representative government?

What is the Federal Government?

The federal government-owned Canada Post delivers about 11 billion pieces of mail a year.

The federal government has power over many issues that concern all provinces and territories. For example, mailing letters in Ontario costs the same as it does in British Columbia. That is because the federal government runs the postal system. A federal government is one of the best ways to govern a country as a whole while protecting the needs of different regions.

Other levels of Canadian government take care of other needs of the people. Provincial and territorial governments handle matters such as education and natural resources. Municipal governments manage things such as emergency services and waste collection and recycling. These two levels of government also make important contributions to running the country.

Powers and Responsibilities in Government

This list shows some of the powers and responsibilities that fall under each level of Canada's three levels of government. Some of these responsibilities are shared.

Federal Government
- taxation (direct and indirect)
- national defence
- regulation of trade and commerce
- foreign policy
- criminal law and procedure
- citizenship and immigration
- employment insurance
- money and banking
- patents and copyrights
- census and statistics
- Indian affairs and Northern development
- postal service

Provincial Government
- direct taxation in the province
- civil law
- provincial courts
- natural resources and environment
- hospitals
- provincial prisons
- social services
- education

The territorial governments (Yukon Territory, Northwest Territories, and Nunavut) have many of the same powers as the provinces. Their powers are not guaranteed by the **Constitution**, however.

Municipal Government
- electric utilities
- economic development
- water and sewage
- emergency services
- libraries
- public transit
- land-use planning
- waste collection and recycling
- animal control

The Federal Government Structure

The federal government is based in Ottawa, Ontario.

In 1867, the British **Parliament** passed the British North American Act, later renamed the Constitution Act. This act united the **colonies** of Nova Scotia, New Brunswick, Ontario, and Quebec. It also gave the new country of Canada a federal government based on Great Britain's parliamentary system.

Canada's parliamentary system includes the House of Commons, the Senate, and the head of state, or **sovereign**. The lower house of Parliament, or the House of Commons, is composed of representatives elected by the people of Canada. Those who serve in the upper house, or the Senate, are appointed to their positions for life. The governor general represents the sovereign, or monarch, who is the queen or king of the United Kingdom. The governor general gives **royal assent** to all laws passed by Parliament.

The federal government of Canada has executive, legislative, and judicial branches. Each branch is responsible for different aspects of running the government. No single branch can abuse its power because the other two can check its activities.

How the Federal Government Works

Canada has a parliamentary system of government with executive, legislative, and judicial branches. Unlike a presidential system, the executive and legislative branches are fused. The executive branch consists of the sovereign, the prime minister, and the cabinet. The legislative branch consists of the sovereign, the Senate, and the House of Commons.

Legislative Branch (Parliament)

Sovereign
Represented in Canada by the governor general

Senate
Appointed on the prime minister's recommendation

House of Commons
Elected by voters

Executive Branch

Prime Minister and Cabinet

Judicial Branch

Supreme Court of Canada

Federal Court of Canada

Provincial Courts

The Executive Branch

Stephen Harper, the 22nd prime minister, made an official visit to Haiti after the 2010 earthquake.

The executive branch is made up of the prime minister and a **cabinet**. The prime minister is head of the government. This person is the leader of the party with the most seats in the House of Commons. The prime minister chooses and leads the cabinet. The prime minister and cabinet direct government policies.

The prime minister and the cabinet
are part of the executive branch.

The cabinet introduces most new legislation. It has the sole power
to prepare and introduce tax legislation and laws related to
spending public money.

About 30 members of Parliament are appointed to the
cabinet to serve as advisers to the prime minister.
The prime minister often selects cabinet
ministers from each province to
encourage fair representation.

Most cabinet ministers are in
charge of specific government
departments, such as finance,
foreign affairs, or the environment.
Cabinet ministers are accountable
to the House of Commons.
Ministers must support the
decisions and policies of the cabinet.

In 1867, John A. Macdonald became
the first prime minister of Canada.

The Legislative Branch

The legislative branch debates proposed laws and then votes on them. This branch is made up of two houses. The elected assembly is called the House of Commons. The appointed body is known as the Senate.

The House of Commons is the most important lawmaking body in Canada. It is made up of 308 members of Parliament, or MPs. Each MP represents the people in his or her electoral district, or **riding**. Canada has been divided into 308 ridings since 2004. Each riding has about the same population. Each province and territory is represented by a set number of MPs.

The legislative branch of the federal government passes laws for the entire country.

Most MPs belong to a **political party**, such as the Liberal Party, the Conservative Party, the New Democratic Party, or the Bloc Québécois. MPs associated with no party are called independents.

Generally, the governing party stays in power as long as it wins a **majority** of seats in the House of Commons in each election. If another political party wins a majority in the House of Commons, the cabinet from the governing party resigns. Then, the governor general calls on the leader of the new **majority party** to form a government. The new prime minister chooses cabinet ministers, who are then formally appointed by the governor general.

The monarch or the governor general traditionally addresses Parliament from the Senate Chamber, also called the Red Chamber.

If no political party receives a majority of seats, the cabinet has two choices. One, the cabinet ministers can resign. In this case, the governor general will call on the leader of the largest opposition party to form a cabinet. Two, the cabinet can choose to stay in office and lead with what is called a **minority government**. In either situation, MPs in the newly elected House of Commons decide whether a minority government stays in office or is replaced.

The floor of the House of Commons has been covered with carpet to improve the sound quality of the chamber during debate.

Sometimes a government loses a vote of confidence, or support, in the House of Commons. In this case, it must either resign or ask the governor general to dissolve Parliament and call an election. If the government resigns, then the **official opposition**, the party with the second-highest number of seats in the House of Commons, forms a government.

The Judicial Branch

A third branch of government is the judicial branch. This branch is made up of the court system and judges. Canada has many levels in its court system. The federal government has control over criminal law and procedure. Provinces have control of the administration of justice in their province.

The highest court in Canada is called the Supreme Court. It determines whether laws agree with or violate Canada's Constitution. This court, which meets in Ottawa, is the final court of appeals.

The Supreme Court of Canada, which meets in Ottawa, hears about 80 appeals a year.

The Supreme Court is made up of nine judges, including the **chief justice**. Under Canadian law, the governor general appoints all Supreme Court justices. However, the prime minister usually suggests candidates to the governor general. By law, at least three people from Quebec must serve on the court. The remaining six positions are usually filled by three judges from Ontario, two from the western provinces, and one from the Atlantic provinces. A Supreme Court justice serves until he or she retires or reaches the age of 75.

The Supreme Court's rulings affect decisions made by other courts. Sometimes, the Supreme Court refuses to rule on a matter if the legislation is not clear. The government is then asked to create new legislation. This process acts as a check on the power of the legislative and executive branches.

Below the Supreme Court is the Federal Court of Canada. It deals mainly with federal tax laws, copyrights, claims against the federal government, and claims from federal statutes. Federal judges are appointed mostly by the minister of justice and sometimes by the prime minister.

There are also often three levels of provincial and territorial courts. Cases that come up through these courts can also be appealed to the Supreme Court of Canada.

Beverley McLachlin was appointed chief justice of the Supreme Court of Canada in 2000. She is the first woman to hold this honour.

Passing Bills in the Legislature

Passing legislation starts with the proposal, formulation, and drafting of a bill.

Passing **bills** is one of the legislative branch's most important tasks. A bill is a draft of a proposed law. The cabinet introduces proposed laws. Legislators study, debate, alter, and vote on bills before they become laws. Both the House of Commons and the Senate must pass all federal laws.

Two types of legislation can be introduced into Parliament. Private bills affect a single person or company. They are fairly uncommon. Most private bills are introduced in the Senate. Public bills concern public policy. These bills affect all or a particular group of Canadians.

In most cases, a cabinet minister introduces a public bill, usually called a government bill, in the House of Commons. All parties in the House of Commons usually debate public bills at length. Sometimes, a member who is not part of the cabinet introduces a public bill. This is called a private member's bill. Private members' bills are often used to pressure the government into action.

How a Bill Is Passed to Become Law

For a bill to pass, it must go through several stages, or readings. Every bill is read three times in each house. The government must give members two-days' written notice before a bill is announced.

The First Reading
- The bill's title is announced, usually by the minister responsible for the bill.
- In most cases, the bill is automatically accepted. It is then printed and distributed.
- There is no debate at this stage.

The Second Reading
- This stage usually occurs a few weeks after the first reading.
- The minister responsible for the bill gives a speech in support of the new law.
- Members debate the principle of the bill.
- The bill is sent to a committee for study. The committee may make amendments.
- The committee's work is sent back to the House of Commons in the report stage.

In the second reading, the committee may alter the bill.

The Third Reading
- The House of Commons reviews the committee's recommendations. It may make amendments.
- Members have another chance to debate the bill.
- The House of Commons votes on the bill. If the bill passes, it is referred to the Senate. There, it undergoes a similar process.
- If the Senate makes any changes to a bill before passing it, the House of Commons must review those changes. The House of Commons can amend the changes and send the bill back to the Senate.

Royal Assent
- Once the bill has passed in both houses in exactly the same form, the governor general signs it in a special ceremony in the Senate chambers. The bill has then received royal assent and becomes law.

The governor general gives royal assent to all bills passed in Parliament. Michaëlle Jean served as governor general until 2010.

Key People in the Federal Government

The Prime Minister

The prime minister is the leader of the country. As leader of the party in power, the prime minister is head of the government. In Canada, the role of the prime minister carries a great deal of power and responsibility. The prime minister selects the cabinet, and with a majority government, controls laws that are proposed and passed in the House of Commons. The prime minister also advises the governor general on the appointment of senators, the Speaker of the Senate, and Supreme Court justices.

Stephen Harper became prime minister of Canada in 2006.

Members of Parliament

The 308 citizens elected to the House of Commons are called members of Parliament, or MPs. MPs are responsible to their voters. Government MPs belong to the party in power. The MPs in the party with the second-highest number of seats in the House of Commons form the official opposition. The Speaker of the House of Commons, elected by sitting MPs, presides over debates. The Speaker votes only to break a tie.

The Cabinet

The MPs appointed to the cabinet serve as advisers to the prime minister. They are responsible for running government departments. Cabinet ministers oversee the work of the civil service. They sometimes resign if a serious problem occurs in their department. Cabinet ministers must support all cabinet decisions or resign.

The Official Opposition

Opposite the prime minister is the leader of the official opposition. He or she is usually the leader of the party with the second-highest number of seats in the House of Commons. This leader chooses a team of party members to study various issues and monitor the work of the governing party. It is called a shadow cabinet.

Michael Ignatieff of the Liberal Party was named opposition leader in 2008.

Senators

Citizens appointed to the Senate are called senators. They study and pass laws prepared by the House of Commons. Senators may serve until the age of 75. A fixed number of senators from each province and territory total 105. They represent the interests of their province or territory. The Speaker of the Senate directs Senate business and is allowed to vote.

The Governor General

The governor general represents the British monarch in Canada. The governor general has mainly social and ceremonial duties. The governor general opens and closes Parliament and gives royal assent to bills in order to make them law. The governor general must follow the advice of the cabinet.

David Johnston was named governor general in 2010.

The Sovereign

If the British monarch, or sovereign, is present, he or she carries out all the duties of the governor general. The sovereign appoints the governor general, based on the advice of the prime minister.

Queen Elizabeth II is head of state for Canada and 14 other Commonwealth realms, as well as the United Kingdom.

Parliament Hill

About three million people visit Parliament Hill every year.

Members of the Canadian government meet at Parliament Hill to make national decisions. Parliament Hill is located in Ottawa, Ontario.

The three Parliament buildings are called the East Block, West Block, and Centre Block. In the East Block are senators' offices and rooms re-created in the style of the early years of Confederation. The West Block houses the offices of ministers, members of Parliament, and their employees.

The Centre Block contains the two chambers where the Senate and the House of Commons meet, as well as the Library of Parliament. The Senate Chamber is found in the east end of the Centre Block. The House of Commons is in the west end. Here, government leaders from across Canada discuss and make laws.

The House of Commons has two sides. One side is for the party in power, and the other side is for the opposition. Between the Senate Chamber and the House of Commons is the Hall of Honour and Confederation Hall. The Library of Parliament is at the end of the Hall of Honour.

The 92.2-metre Peace Tower is named in honour of the men and women who gave their lives for their country in World War I. Inside the Peace Tower is the Memorial Chamber. The Chamber honours Canada's war dead. Its floor is made of stones collected from battlegrounds.

Floor Plan of the Centre Block

The mission of the Library of Parliament is to create, manage, and deliver reliable and relevant information for Parliament.

The Hall of Honour is used for state occasions, parliamentary events, and formal processions.

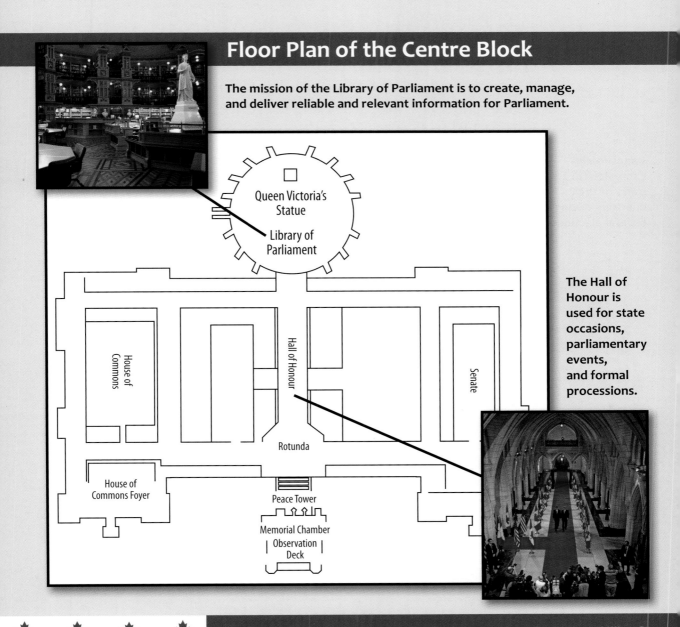

The Election Process

Federal elections take place usually about every four years. By law, parliamentary elections must be held at least once every five years. However, if the government loses the confidence of the House of Commons, an election can be called sooner.

Elections give citizens a chance to review the work of their political leaders. Citizens can help determine whether a leader should continue or be replaced. They inform themselves about the candidates, the parties, and the issues.

Federal elections require a minimum of 36 campaign days. There is no maximum of campaign days. However, Parliament must meet at least once every 12 months. Federal elections always take place on a Monday. If the Monday is a statutory holiday, the election takes place the following Tuesday.

People often campaign for the party of their choosing during federal elections.

The Canada Elections Act outlines who is allowed to run in a federal election. A candidate must be a Canadian citizen who is 18 years old on election day. He or she must also be nominated by at least 100 voters in his or her riding. Candidates are required to pay a deposit of $1,000, which is reimbursed only if the candidate receives at least 10 percent of the vote in his or her district. Most successful candidates belong to a major political party.

How to Vote

Voters must be Canadian citizens who are 18 years or older on election day. They must live in the district in which they are voting. The steps for the voting process are below.

1. Confirm that your name appears on the voter list. If you are not on the voter list, you can register during a 28-day period before the election, at an advance polling station, or at a polling station on election day. You may also choose to vote during the advance polls or by special mail-in **ballot**.

2. You will receive a voter information card with the address of your polling station. If you do not receive a voter information card, call the **returning officer** in your electoral district.

3. Next, you will go to your polling station on election day. After showing proof of your identity and address, you will get a ballot paper.

4. At the polling station, you will vote by secret ballot in a private polling booth. To vote, you need to make a clear mark in the box by the name of the candidate you prefer.

5. Once you have voted, you will give your ballot to a polling station official. That person will put it into a ballot box.

6. The paper ballots are counted after the polls close. All federal elections use paper ballots. Using an electronic voting process would require approval from committees in Parliament.

7. The official results of the count are announced to the public.

Facts to Know

Elections Canada determines the electoral districts for federal elections. The chief electoral officer for Canada determines the number of seats for each province and territory based on population and legislation. The map below shows Canada's 308 electoral districts.

UNITED STATES

N

0   500 Kilometres

Yukon Territory
1

Northwest Territories
1

Nunavut
1

British Columbia
36

C A N A D A

Alberta
28

Manitoba
14

Newfoundland and Labrador
7

Saskatchewan
14

Ontario
106

Quebec
75

Prince Edward Island
4

New Brunswick
10

Nova Scotia
11

UNITED STATES

Election Poll Hours

A polling station's hours of operation are set so that the majority of results come in at about the same time, regardless of time zone. The map below shows the hours for polling stations across Canada. Some districts have more than one time zone. In this case, the returning officer receives the approval of the chief electoral officer to set one local time for the entire district.

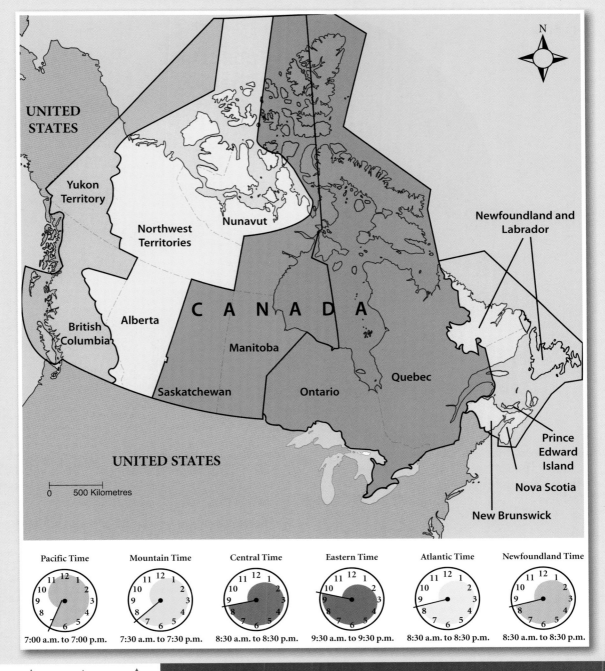

In the budget year from April 2007 through March 2008, the federal government received $242.4 billion in taxes and other revenues. This pie chart shows how a federal tax dollar was spent.

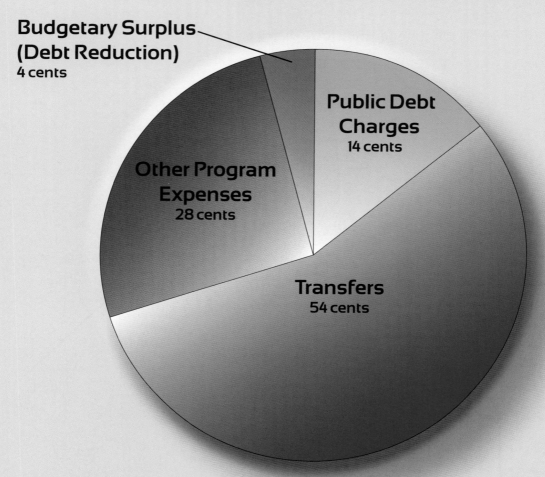

Budgetary Surplus (Debt Reduction)
4 cents

Public Debt Charges
14 cents

Other Program Expenses
28 cents

Transfers
54 cents

Public debt charges are interest payments on Canada's public debt. These are payments to institutions and people who hold federal bonds, treasury bills, and other forms of the debt. These charges were $33.3 billion.

Transfers are payments made to individuals, organizations, and provincial and territorial governments. Old Age Security and employment insurance payments are two types of transfers. The federal government also provides funding for programs in the provinces and territories, such as health care, post-secondary education, and social assistance. These payments totalled $131.3 billion.

Other program expenses include defence, public safety, federal government operations, and the Canada Revenue Agency, which regulates income tax. These expenses were $68.2 billion.

Budgetary surplus is how much money is left after paying for all federal programs, operations, and interest on the debt. This surplus is not available for future spending. Any surplus at year-end automatically reduces the federal debt. This number equalled $9.6 billion.

Prime Ministers of Canada

Canada has had many prime ministers since its founding. The list below shows their years of service and party affiliation.

TERM	PRIME MINISTER	PARTY
1867–1873	Sir John A. Macdonald	Liberal-Conservative
1873–1878	Alexander Mackenzie	Liberal
1878–1891	Sir John A. Macdonald	Liberal-Conservative
1891–1892	Sir John J. C. Abbott	Liberal-Conservative
1892–1894	Sir John S. D. Thompson	Liberal-Conservative
1894–1896	Sir Mackenzie Bowell	Conservative
1896	Sir Charles Tupper	Conservative
1896–1911	Sir Wilfrid Laurier	Liberal
1911–1917	Sir Robert Borden	Conservative
1917–1920	Sir Robert Borden	Unionist Coalition (Conservative/Liberal)
1920–1921	Arthur Meighen	Unionist Coalition (Conservative/Liberal)
1921–1926	William Lyon Mackenzie King	Liberal
1926	Arthur Meighen	Conservative
1926–1930	William Lyon Mackenzie King	Liberal
1930–1935	Richard B. Bennett	Conservative
1935–1948	William Lyon Mackenzie King	Liberal
1948–1957	Louis St. Laurent	Liberal
1957–1963	John Diefenbaker	Progressive Conservative
1963–1968	Lester B. Pearson	Liberal
1968–1979	Pierre E. Trudeau	Liberal
1979–1980	Charles Joe Clark	Progressive Conservative
1980–1984	Pierre E. Trudeau	Liberal
1984	John Turner	Liberal
1984–1993	Brian Mulroney	Progressive Conservative
1993	Kim Campbell	Progressive Conservative
1993–2003	Jean Chrétien	Liberal
2003–2006	Paul Martin	Liberal
2006–	Stephen Harper	Conservative

Activities

Hold a Democratic Meeting

Think about how the following story relates to Canada's system of government.

A woman sat on the beach with her children while her husband built a log cabin in the woods. Animals from the nearby woods gathered to watch the family. They grew worried about how these people would affect their lives.

Birds, bears, deer, squirrels, coyotes, and all the other woodland animals gathered together one day to debate the issue. Cougar, acting as king of the forest, called the meeting to order. Each animal group shared its opinions. Some animals feared the family would hunt them for their meat or fur. Other animals enjoyed the family's scraps of food. The family's dog explained that the family would not hunt the animals and might help warm and feed them in winter. The animals analyzed the various opinions. They understood how they could view the same issue in many ways. After this discussion, some of the animals changed their minds. Other animals felt the same way as when the meeting started.

After much debate, they voted on whether to allow the people to stay in the woods or to drive them away. In the end, six animal groups voted to drive the people away while seven animal groups voted to let the people stay. Most of the animals agreed to live among the family. Animals that did not agree could leave the woods if they wanted.

Choose an issue with two sides, and hold your own democratic meeting. Let a representative from each side explain its view and give any important facts. Also let each side respond to the other side's arguments. Then let the group vote on a solution. How did you feel about the issue before the meeting? Did your feelings change or stay the same as a result of the debate?

Conduct a Mock Election

All citizens of Canada who meet the requirements can run for federal office. Try hosting a mock election to learn more about the election process.

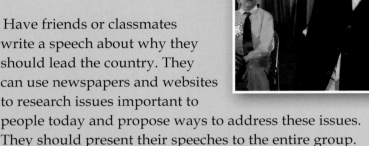

1. Have friends or classmates write a speech about why they should lead the country. They can use newspapers and websites to research issues important to people today and propose ways to address these issues. They should present their speeches to the entire group.

2. After hearing the speeches, have your friends or classmates nominate candidates for election.

3. Candidates have one week to campaign. During this time, they might hang posters, hand out fliers, or make presentations to convince people to vote for them.

4. Host a question-and-answer period. Have all of the candidates sit at the front of the group while friends and classmates ask them questions.

5. On election day, hand out ballots to each member of the group. Ballots should have each candidate listed next to "yes" and "no" boxes. Voters should check the "yes" box for their preferred candidate and check the "no" box for all other candidates. Then, they should fold the ballot and place it inside the ballot box.

6. Count all of the ballots. If any ballots have a check mark in more than one "yes" box or have been filled out incorrectly, the vote does not count. The person with the most check marks in the "yes" box wins the election.

WHAT Have You LEARNED?

Answer these questions to see what you have learned about Canada's federal government.

1 What term describes Canada's democracy?

2 What are the three levels of government in Canada?

3 What is it called when the governor general signs a bill?

4 Who is the official opposition leader?

5 Where do members of the federal government meet?

6 What is Canada's highest court?

7 What are the three branches of federal government?

8 How many federal electoral districts does Canada have?

9 Who does the governor general represent in Canada?

10 What are the two types of legislation that can be introduced in Parliament?

ANSWERS: 1. *Representative democracy* 2. *Federal, provincial/territorial, and municipal* 3. *Royal assent* 4. *The leader of the party that received the second-highest number of seats in an election* 5. *Parliament Hill in Ottawa, Ontario* 6. *The Supreme Court of Canada* 7. *Executive, legislative, and judicial* 8. *308* 9. *The British monarch* 10. *Public bills and private bills*

Find Out More

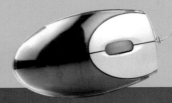

Many books and websites provide information on the federal government. To learn more about the federal government, borrow books from the library or do research online.

BOOKS

Most libraries have computers with an online catalog. If you input a key word, you will get a list of related books in the library. Nonfiction books are arranged numerically by call number. Fiction books are organized alphabetically by the author's last name.

WEBSITES

Libraries often have online reference databases that you can access from any computer. You can also use an Internet search engine, but be sure to verify the source of the website's information. Official websites run by government agencies are usually reliable, for example. To find out more about the federal government, type key words, such as "Canada's system of government," "Canada's House of Commons," or "Canada's Senate," into the search field.

Words to Know

ballot: a ticket or sheet of paper used to cast a vote

bills: proposed laws

cabinet: a group of members of Parliament chosen by the prime minister to head government departments and to develop policies and plans to govern the country

chief justice: the justice who is the official head of a supreme court

colonies: areas that are not independent but are controlled by a foreign state

constitution: the fundamental principles and rules under which a country is governed

direct democracy: a form of government that gives every citizen the right to vote on every issue

majority: more than half of a total

majority government: a government in which more than one half of the elected seats belong to the political party in power

minority government: a government whose party has fewer than half the seats in the House of Commons

official opposition: generally, the party with the second-highest number of seats in the House of Commons

Parliament: a lawmaking body; Parliament in Canada is composed of the House of Commons, the Senate, and the monarchy

political party: a group of people who share similar ideas about how government should operate

representative democracy: a form of government in which citizens do not take part directly but elect representatives to pass laws and make decisions on behalf of everyone

returning officer: the person in charge of the election in a particular riding

riding: an electoral district represented by a member of Parliament or of a provincial or territorial legislature

royal assent: the formal signing of an act of Parliament by which it becomes law

sovereign: the monarch who serves as head of state

INDEX